# Behind the Scenes

Amy Schneiderman

BookLeaf Publishing

India | USA | UK

Presentation by *BookLeaf Publishing*

Web: www.bookleafpub.com

E-mail: info@bookleafpub.com

ISBN: 9789360943936

First edition 2024

# sunrise

above a meadow
green and red; the sun yellow.
purple clouds up high.

sharp. sterile. stunning.

end of the night.
beginning of the day. means
a fresh start today.

# Perfect

you're not flawed,
even if society says so.
they may have broken barriers
and put words in your head, so.
hear how I say you're not flawed,
you're you. perfect in every way

and if society denies it.
tell them you're not buying it.
because all the flaws
that make up you
make you,
in every way,
Perfect.

# Together

Two years
is a long time ago.
We met
a long time ago.
Through little moments
odds and ends
All those moments
Blurred together
into memories like they were yesterday

I'll never forget how
lunch was always better with you.
how in a sea of sophomore strangers
you were a smiling familiar face.
how we sat on the table
during the movie in class.
how you made a video
with a picture of something I wrote.
how I cried and you held me,
and you cried, and I held you.

Summer was hell. I almost fell.
but among the ones holding the rope
throwing it down into the well,
there was you.

And I forgot.
Most of the memories. but that's okay.
because I'm still here.
with you.

We had lunch together again,
We sat in my favorite teacher's room.
We fed the turtles together
and I don't remember how it came to be,
but when we say goodbye,
we always say it our way
with our secret handshake.
Then your heart broke,
mine hated seeing yours in pain.
Then my world shattered,
I had to say goodbye to him
it wasn't fair,
but through it all,
you were there.

This year,
we found a new hiding spot,
we thought it was impenetrable
…until we got caught.
and after school that monday,
we explored the hidden stairway.
and when we cry, we know what to do
we know each other better now.
and today it still rings true,

lunch is always better with you.

It's crazy to think
how come May,
we'll be graduating.
And it's crazy to think
how come summer's end,
we'll be going our separate ways.

I don't want this year to end,
but I do.
I want to find my next chapter,
but I want my every waking moment,
to be with you.

And it's hard
for me to say,
hard
for my heart to hear,
but without you is okay.
The memories fall like snow,
moments flurry around me.
We'll never end;
We'll keep going
Just…
in a different way

# panic attack

you're underwater
in a cage
sharks swim around you
but they can't get you
you try to call out
to the world above
but the signal gets lost
and you're running out of air
you know you should conserve it
breathe deep, calm down
but the more you try
the harder it gets
this feels fatal now
feels like the KO blow now
feels like you're all alone now
the surface gets further and
further away
until
it's all gone
and you're afraid
the sharks are getting brave
and your air is all you have to live on
and pretty soon it'll be done
and you're falling deeper down
but a hand reaches out

and pulls you up
and this whole time
you
were in
your
bedroom

# let go

there's too many people.
who don't know.
or won't get it.
if they were told.

it's too loud;
I should get my headphones.
the noise hurts
my brain, my ears
like a thousand nails on chalkboards
all at the same time
only I could hear.
but there's too many people.

it's too hot;
I wish I could change.
I can't let it go
the way it works its way
up and through
infects my brain
like water running down the drain
it's cold outside, but
inside?
it's too hot.

and I wonder what would happen
if I let go
of the popsicle stick
I hold
the one that holds a paper
with a smiley face
it does such a nice job
covering my face.

I try,
to take it off,
but it's stuck.
glued in place.

there's too many people.
who don't know.
or won't get it.
if they were told.

# Mirror

in the sky,
up so high

the clouds part way
for an airplane

brilliant, blue
wonderful, true

all the trees look up
wishing they could touch

but while everyone sure is in envy
the airplane doesn't see their excellency

and when people try to tell
they make words bounce off their shell

if the airplane could see
maybe they would agree

agree they're not so bad
in fact, they're kinda rad

but the plane won't hear-maybe out of fear

they really want to believe
but it's easier to leave

so they ask family and friends
to write words that will help them mend

and they up pin motivating notes to their
windshield
thinking it'll be good; thinking it'll help them
heal

and now instead of wishing to crash.
they only laugh
and now instead of thinking they're a weight.
they look up to the sky,
oh, so high,
and know they're a wing-
the best of kinds

# How To Be A Lottie

12

never walk in rain
always let your voice be heard
always be real cute

# the squirrel

13

noteworthy squirrel
look at you climbing the wall
so cute as you do
look at you climbing the tree
you climb so elegantly

# playdate

14

if a cat came up to me today,
and asked me if I wanted to play,
I wouldn't say no
it's a crime to do so!
so I guess I'd be stuck all day!

# The Butterfly Effect

It's the butterfly effect
it draws you in
and flaps its wings
and then, suddenly,
before you even have time to think -
to blink,
it wraps you up in its warm embrace
and your life is changed forever.

Forget what you knew
forget what you know
none of that matters now
This world is a whole new world
and you are a stranger in a strange land.

So you draw your sword
and unsheathe your feathered pen
but wait - it's the butterfly effect
one wrong move and this whole new world will
end.

But this is your story
you can't die
the hero never dies
so you think to yourself

in this whole new world
are you the hero?
or the villain?

And if you are the hero,
why are you the hero?
you did nothing to deserve this.
you are not worthy.
so you lay down your sword
and your feathered pen
and think to yourself;

And if you are the villain,
what did you do to deserve this?
you did nothing wrong.
or at least you think you didn't.

So you are neither the hero nor the villain
you pick up your feathered pen
and in this strange,
large,
scary,
whole new world
you choose to pave your own path
make your own mark
write your own story.

This world is not all that scary anymore
you are no longer the hero,

nor the villain.
in this brave new world.

In silence you realize, you are not nothing
You are you
You are beautiful and true
And that's all that matters.

# Live On

A flower blooms in a desert,
not far from here.

A fire burns on a ship,
one that's just parted the pier.

The flower is strong,
it has a will to survive.
The fire burns bright,
it has a love of being alive.

It's a symbiotic relationship,
what they've created.
It's something hard to replicate,
never to be traded.

Years after the flowers gone,
and its seeds live on
Years after the fire's been snuffed out,
and its ashes been thrown out

A caterpillar hangs on a tree,
one where the flower's seeds used to be.
Across the room,
a new fire fumes.

As the caterpillar comes out of its shell,
and greets the world for the first time
it feels the fire,
and is ready to unleash the beauty inside.

# Falling Over Time

It's written on the sky
The way time will fly
You'll think it's got your back,
But it doesn't
It's nothing but a traitor
It'll hold you in it's soft embrace
Until you feel

        secure

you won't feel

      like you can

            f
            a
            l
            l
            but you can
            and you will

When the night comes to an end,
    you won't ever
       feel the same way

       Again.

# The Fallen Rocket

After the rocket fell
Before the heat of the moment
Caged was my heart
Destroyed was my life and
Extreme was my pain. Tell me how could I
Forget your smile and
Go about life without you
Here. You weren't my lover, but you were the
light of my light and
I know time has to go on but
Joke's on me, because I
Know I can't wait for you
Like I'd like to, and every time I see your
picture on
My wall, with you doing all the things you
shouldn't, my heart drops just a little bit more
and
Now I search for you in every scene I see
Oceans of walls, it doesn't matter where. I turn
the
Page and it's the climax. The part where
characters
Quarrel and turn on each other. The part where
heartbreak
Reins supreme and

Suffice it to say I'll never stop missing you. Not when
The oceans stop turning and the rivers stop moaning, and when I'm
Under the stars, I'll look up, wave at you, and wait until the
Voice of fallacy that took you from me admits I'm right. It's
Wrong. Put an
X-ray against my skin, you'll see my heart beat,
Yearning for the days when you'd
Zoom through the house, and I'd laugh like it was just us in this world

# miss you <3

23

I miss you, on me
you were the king of my dreams.
I love the way you
drove the rain and pain away,
all I needed? you near me.

# DOOMED WITHOUT YOU

If it weren't for you
This world would be doomed
An apocalyptic type show
With crumbling brick and loose stones
Roll the film back twice
You'll see it play in black and white

If it weren't for you
in your purple nightgown
This world would be doomed
A flooded over beach
With me drowning and your hand just
A dash out of reach
Remember when I screamed:
"You don't love me at all!"
I'd take it all back now,
If you'd teach me how not to fall

If it weren't for your laugh
urging the flowers to bloom
This world would be doomed
Dull, lifeless, and without color
With hearts written in stars,
never quite touching each other

If not for every failed flight,
Or tears showing us how to write
There would've been
no laughter last night

Without you,
This world would be doomed
Dark and dilapidated,
With a desolate future
I'd run wild,
hands in the air
Lost is what I'd be
Without you

If it weren't for you and the sky stained blue
If it weren't for you and the love that feels too
good to be true
If it weren't for you and me, the flower who
refused to bloom
If it weren't for you and all the fearless colors
that make up you
If it weren't for you, my world would be
doomed

If it weren't for you
This world would be doomed
An apocalyptic type show
With crumbling brick and loose stones
Roll the film back twice

You'll see it play in full colors
of beautiful flaws starlit in the limelight

26

# THANK YOU

27

This is to you, who
Helps me through
All the hell and stays by my side
No matter what, always with pride. you, who
Knows me like a cat lands on their feet.

You, who can read me like a book and can
always tell when I'm
Overwhelmed and overstimulated. This is to
you; the
Unrivaled.

# Through Thick & Thin

I might gift you a stuffed cat
or I might adopt a real cat
and give it to you
because I know you've always wanted one

I might give you a birthday card
or I might write a poem
dedicated to you
because you mean so much to me

I might just hug you
or I might fall into you
after the hug's been completed
because I know you'll always catch me

I might hold you close when you cry
pick something carefree to talk about
to get you to smile; laugh
to get your mind off what made you sad

I might be playful as a panda
and curious as a kitten;
but through thick and thin,
I'm by your side.

# Rise

heat rises
balloons rise
and birds fly

age rises
bubbles rise
and bats fly

tide rises
squids can fly;
why can't I?

# sunset

30

sun pierces the waves,
like looking in a mirror,
clouds mimic water.

sharp. sterile. stunning.

a moment like this
know you better capture it
lest you forget it.